Foreword by Alan Titchmarsh

The Great Outdoors

My own interest in gardening began when I was v[illegible] always what I liked to do best. I'm delighted that through my television work especially, many more children are becoming interested and involved in gardening for themselves, and I hope that children today will be able to enjoy it as much as I always have done.

When I think back to being in the garden in Yorkshire as a lad, I remember that just being outside had as much to offer as actual gardening. The fresh air was good, there was freedom and space to muck about with my friends, to run, climb, and ride my bike. I could be noisy, make dens, get filthy dirty and use my imagination. I loved playing out on the moors, down by the river, in the bluebell woods – and getting out of my parents' hair and giving them a bit of peace.

Just like me then, children today need the time, freedom and space to play outside. Gardens are a good place for this, and playing in them must not be frowned on for the sake of keeping a border untrampled. Plants and children both need space to grow. Where children don't have access to gardens of their own, parks, recreation grounds, village greens and other open spaces are a good alternative, and play areas in playgroups, nurseries and schools should be developed as much as possible.

Children these days are not as physically active as they were in my childhood, and they seem to have even less free time of their own. It is therefore more important than ever that all those who work with children take outdoor opportunities seriously. My 'Gardens for Schools' project is helping to fund primary schools to create or improve school gardens, but I am also keen to encourage children to do what they are naturally very good at, namely playing and enjoying all the opportunities offered by the 'Great Outdoors'. There's nowhere like it.

Contents

Introduction

Many adults fondly remember the time they spent out of doors as children. This booklet explains why outdoor experiences are essential for development and learning, and highlights some of the opportunities children need.

It is written for all those who spend time with young children as parent, carer, childminder, play-worker, nursery nurse, teacher or classroom assistant. It explores why it is important for children to learn out of doors and identifies how practitioners and parents can support children's development in this area.

Throughout the booklet, adults working with children in early years settings, play-workers and childminders, are referred to as 'practitioners'. Those who are significant carers for children at home are referred to as 'parents'.

What is outdoor learning? Why is it important?

When adults are asked what they can remember about being out of doors as children, they nearly all recall a similar range of experiences. Whether they grew up in towns, cities or villages, in the United Kingdom or in other parts of the world, they nearly all remember being given a great deal of freedom. Many talk about being outside most of the time. Comments such as 'I can't remember what I did indoors; all my memories are outdoor ones', are very common. Children from whole streets regularly played together. This meant that children were mixing across a wide age range, with older children trusted to take responsibility for younger ones. Often children roamed far away from home, only returning for food or sleep!

When asked to recall what they did out of doors, adults talk about:

- imaginative play such as making dens in hedges, trees or with an old clotheshorse and sheet, or playing 'Cowboys and Indians', superheroes, mums and dads, shops, hospitals and much more. Props for imaginative play were readily available; natural found and borrowed items such as leaves or sticks, mum's old clothes, a dustbin lid or broom. These items were often used for different purposes, depending on the play and the player combinations
- messy play with natural materials such as mud pies, making perfume with rose petals or damming streams
- construction play with sticks, logs, boxes, stones or bricks and old blankets or cloths
- games with rules such as hide and seek, jacks, hopscotch
- physical play such as climbing trees, riding bikes, chasing each other, roller-skating, playing ball, learning to use a hula hoop.

Adults recognise that these outdoor experiences were important in shaping their development as a person and as a learner. They say it:

- helped them develop positive relationships with others; learning to put forward their ideas, share, take turns and negotiate
- supported the development of communication and language and

literacy skills for example, when reading and writing messages or instructions left by others
- developed their self-confidence and gave a sense of achievement, awe and wonder
- developed physical strength and skill and gave a sense of physical well-being; it is important to remember that children will only be able to control and co-ordinate their hands and feet if they have developed control of their arms and legs. Control is necessary for skills such as using pencils and scissors, or kicking a ball accurately
- encouraged them to be independent, take responsibility and to make choices
- enabled them to assess risk and develop an understanding of what is, and is not, wise behaviour
- enhanced their knowledge of the natural world including names of plants and awareness of seasonal features and changes
- developed mathematical skills such as counting, estimating, calculating, measuring
- encouraged creativity, use of imagination, problem solving strategies and resourcefulness.

In other words their outdoor play offered them a rich curriculum.

In considering the benefits of outdoor experience, it becomes obvious that some things can only be learnt out of doors, such as learning about nature, the seasons or weather conditions. Everything else has the potential to be learnt out of doors just as effectively as indoors. In fact some children are more likely to learn out of doors, particularly those with a more active kinaesthetic learning style. These are more likely to be boys.

Adults recognise that children's experience today is very different from their own childhoods. Increased traffic, the heightened fear of abduction often fuelled by the media, and the advent of television, videos and computer games has meant that children growing up today have little opportunity to play freely out of doors with their siblings, friends and neighbours. Even those children with gardens may not be able to play in them. Garden makeover programmes on television have encouraged landscaping that is often adult, rather than child-friendly.

The increasingly sedentary nature of young children's lives is leading to serious concern for their health. A growing number of under- fives are already overweight, or even obese, due to poor diet and lack of exercise. According to the Coronary Prevention Group, some children as young as three are already exhibiting signs that they are at risk of heart disease in later life. There are also concerns for children's emotional health. Where adults are overly fearful and try to foresee, and protect their children from all risk, children are prevented from learning important life skills. When they later have to be given some freedom, many are unable to cope, make decisions or be in control. Some may be over-fearful themselves, while others may become wild or reckless.

Within the context of outdoor opportunities for children, it is more and more important that early years settings, practitioners and schools should encourage full use, by children, of their outside areas. If adults comment that 'I didn't spend much time outside when I was at school and it didn't do me any harm', they must recognise that in their own childhoods their non-school based time was more predominantly outdoors and it is even likely that they may have started school at a later age than children today, especially in the UK. Outdoor learning makes a major contribution to children's development. Young children will be missing out on important learning opportunities if quality outdoor provision is not available to them regularly.

Children developing in the great outdoors. What do they need?

Essentially children need a range of outdoor experiences similar to those adults remember and enjoyed as children. They need:

- space to be physically active and to develop and refine the full range of large and smaller movements
- time to observe, explore and become fascinated by the natural world
- quiet spaces to be reflective and watch the world go by, or to sit and talk to a friend
- opportunity to play with their friends and get involved in imagining, creating, constructing, problem-solving and communicating with each other
- a chance to use materials and resources in ways which are not possible indoors
- realistic challenges for physical, social, emotional and intellectual development which help them to develop a sense of themselves as capable achievers
- support from empathetic adults who can help them make connections in their learning and who support and extend their ideas
- suitable clothing and footwear which enables them to move freely and safely and to experience a range of weather conditions. As the Scandinavians say 'There is no such thing as bad weather, only unsuitable clothing'!

Above all children need adults who understand their need for outdoor opportunities and are enthusiastic about sharing their experiences. Practitioners must help the adults they come into contact with to value quality outdoor provision for children.

What can practitioners do to develop outdoor provision?

Getting started

Practitioners work in a wide range of settings which do not all have readily accessible outdoor provision. The starting point for development is therefore to consider what outside spaces are available and evaluate the strengths and weaknesses of these. Those with no, or only a small amount of outdoor provision will need to think about their wider community and identify parks or other outdoor spaces they may be able to access. Having identified strengths and weaknesses, teams need to highlight those weaknesses they can do nothing about such as the too small area which cannot be made bigger. There is no point in focusing on something which cannot be changed. It is better to preserve energy for those things something can be done about, for example, the ugly wall that could be brightened up by a mural or by strategically positioned hanging baskets. This evaluation will provide practitioners with the start of an action plan for developing their area. Getting the whole community involved at this stage is important. Parents and local businesses may have skills to share, may be willing to supply materials or may organise some fundraising for specific items.

Organising outdoor space

Practitioners need to think about the types of experiences that they wish to offer children out of doors and consider how they will organise space to accommodate these. Most practitioners take a great deal of care when organising the rooms they work in. They think about the areas of provision they want to offer and consider which would go well near each other and which need to be as far apart as possible. They then think about resources and equipment and how to organise these. The same kind of thinking process needs to be applied to outdoor provision, but too often space has not been well thought out and the wheeled toys dominate. If the outside area is of a reasonable size, practitioners should aim to create a range of permanent areas. If the area is small, practitioners will need to rotate areas of provision offering a full range over time. Perhaps for one day or week the area could have a broadly physical focus, followed by an imaginative focus the next day or week. Outdoor areas of provision can be defined by low walls or fences, traffic cones, screens or trellis, or simply a chalk or painted line and could include:

- **a climbing area** – this does not need expensive fixed climbing frames but will need a suitable surface such as bark or rubber. Challenging climbing opportunities can be offered by obstacle courses using resources such as planks, A-Frames, tyres or tunnels. In small areas it is never wise to dominate space with a large permanent structure
- **space to run** – children need to be offered the chance to run vigorously in a large open space. This increases their heart rate and thereby promotes healthy heart development. Settings with very small areas will need to find parks or fields they can take the children to from time to time
- **a defined part of the play area where wheeled vehicles can be ridden** – some settings have road markings or pathways around their playground. Others section off an area for the wheeled toys. It is useful to mark parking bays, preferably sited near the storage shed, so

children know where they can park their vehicle when they have finished using it. Parking bays can sometimes be numbered, or be marked with letters or shapes, to correspond with labels on the vehicles, so children need to match their bike into the relevant space. It is important that children know where vehicles are allowed to go. If there is a vehicle ban in a designated area, such as a climbing area, children are more likely stick to rules willingly when they understand the reason for them, or have been involved in establishing them. For example, it is easy to understand that bikes ridden near climbing areas can be very dangerous for riders, who might get kicked or crash into structures. They are also very dangerous for climbers, who might lose their concentration as they climb, or may even get knocked off by a vehicle

- **space to develop skills with small equipment such as balls, bats, bean-bags hoops and quoits** – if there is a wall facing onto this area, targets could be painted onto it and basket-ball nets attached. Number or alphabet snakes could be chalked or painted on the ground or wall to encourage children to aim a bean-bag at a specified letter or number
- **a quiet area where children can be quiet and reflective** or where younger or more timid children can be protected from the more boisterous ones. This can simply be a blanket or mat in a corner or a set of child-sized garden table and chairs or could be a more elaborate fixed structure. Gazebos or garden umbrellas can be used to provide all-important shade, and planting tubs with herbs or other fragrant plants near the area can develop the children's sense of smell
- **places to hide in** – either natural areas such as a carefully shaped evergreen bush or space in the hedge, or created by staff and children such as a tent or a blanket over a frame or large box
- **a wild area where children can explore the natural world** – this can be a small corner of a grassed area which is fenced off and left to

grow wild, or a large container planted with wild flowers and plants like buddleia which attract butterflies. Practitioners working in schools may be able to access the school's wild area. Some logs or old pieces of carpet on grass will enable children to look carefully underneath for creatures

- **an area for large scale construction and imaginative play**
- **space for play with natural materials such as sand, water and mud**
- **a gardening area where children can grow plants and vegetables authentically** – tubs, hanging baskets or old sinks can be used if no garden space is available.

It is important to remember that outdoor developments take time to plan and that practitioners need persistence, patience and stamina to turn their plans into reality.

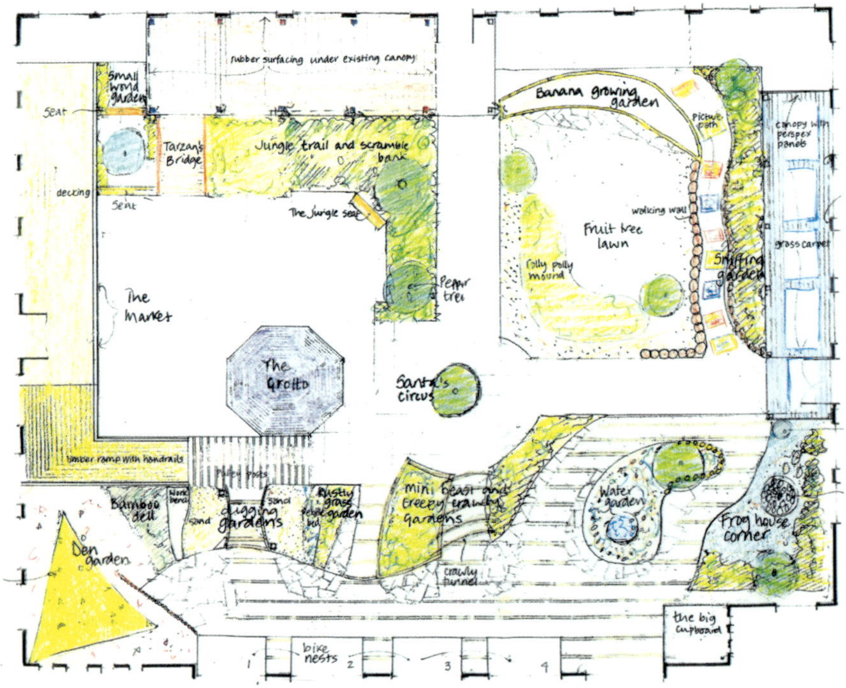

Selecting and organising resources

Resources and equipment used out of doors need to be robust and capable of withstanding heavy use. They should reflect a similar range of opportunities as would be available indoors but should offer children the chance to work on a larger scale than is possible indoors. A range of open-ended resources including tyres, wooden blocks, blankets or sheets to inspire imagination is essential. Children need to be able to use resources in different ways to represent different ideas. It is therefore better not to purchase climbing equipment that looks like something particular such as a train or rocket.

Resources do not have to be expensive. Although some items will be costly others can be obtained for little or no cost.

There are many low or no cost items which can be collected, donated or bought from cheap stores. They include:

milk crates
large pebbles
shells
bakers' trays
recycled boxes
tyres
steering wheels
car number plates
logs
old sinks for planting
hanging baskets
planters
pieces of guttering
plastic piping
hose pipes
rope (washing line)
garden umbrella
camping equipment
blankets/sheets/curtains
large rolls of paper
garden tools
cardboard tubing (e.g. from carpet shops)
umbrellas
wellington boots
waterproof coats and trousers
old cameras
wind chimes
flower pots of different sizes
windmills
seed trays
dressing up hats and clothes
road atlases
clothes horse
large buckets
seeds or cuttings
metal saucepans (for music and sand/water)
picnic set
shopping baskets
suitcases
kites
flags
wood shavings
fishing nets
timetables
tickets
plans of buildings
sheets of plastic or tarpaulin
brooms with handles cut short
storage containers
balls of different sizes made from a variety of materials

It is always important to check with local health and safety advisers to ensure that they consider equipment to be acceptable for use out of doors. Safety requirements vary from one area to another. Whatever resources practitioners use, they need to make regular safety audits to make sure there are no sharp edges or surfaces and that all equipment is still in a good condition.

The following types of resources would offer children a broad outdoor experience:

- **mark-making resources** – a trolley on wheels could be provided which is equipped with such things as paper, clipboards, chalks, crayons, pencils. Children can also make marks with buckets of water and a range of brushes of different sizes. If it is possible to fix a magnet board on a wall, trays of magnetic numbers and letters could be offered to encourage message writing. Sticks in the sand or mud can also encourage more tactile learners to have a go at mark-making. When children are playing scoring games such as skittles, or throwing a bean bag into a bucket, a score sheet could be attached to an easel or clipboard so that children can keep their own score
- **construction resources** – it is worth investing in a large set of wooden hollow blocks as these allow very varied forms of representation. Additionally crates or bakers' trays, tyres, steering wheels and different sized cardboard boxes can be offered to inspire construction. Shoeboxes make good lightweight bricks. A readily available crate or box of old blankets, sheets, curtains and floor tiles will be used to make roofs or carpets for constructions as well as being used for dressing up. Plans of buildings and structures can be made available for children to refer to, and clipboards and pencils sited near the area may encourage children to sketch their buildings and maybe make a plan
- **resources for role-play and imaginative play** – children will set their own imaginative play agendas, particularly where open-ended props are available. However, adults will also want to inspire children to act

out real-life situations or stories. Contexts for imaginative role-play need to be ones which are naturally suited to the outdoors and which reflect the life experience of the children in the group. These contexts might include:

- ambulance
- building site
- bus, railway station or airport
- camping
- car wash
- drive through McDonalds
- farms
- fast food stall
- fire-fighters
- garage
- garden centre
- market stall
- police
- picnic

The list is endless. Stories to be developed out of doors could include The Three Billy Goats Gruff, Percy the Park-Keeper, Bears in the Night and many more. Practitioners will find that is worth developing themed resource boxes containing relevant props and dressing up items so that children's imaginative interests can be followed.

- **natural resources :**

  sand – some early years settings have sand-pits where children can get into the sand. It is also possible to offer this opportunity on a large plastic sheet or tarpaulin or even in a large tractor tyre or builder's tray. Large spades and buckets offer a more challenging experience than is possible with smaller buckets and spades indoors. Sand needs to be covered over when not in use

  water – exciting water play opportunities can be achieved by connecting up pieces of guttering, hose pipe and funnels to fences or along a construction made from milk crates or large blocks. Squeezy bottles come into their own outside and can be used to make trails or to experiment with forces. In summer paddling pools can be enjoyed

mud – there is nothing quite like digging in the mud. With a good supply of Wellington boots, a defined digging patch and some real but child-size garden tools and gardening gloves, children will be able to experience what many of their parents remember so fondly. Like sand, digging patches need to be covered when not in use

other natural resources – full use should also be made of natural resources such as leaves, conkers, shells, large smooth pebbles, wood shavings, bark. These can be used for collage or as habitats for small world play, for example making miniature gardens. If indoor sand trays are taken outside it is better to offer a different material to explore e.g. the tray could be filled with dry leaves, wood shavings or bark

- **resources to develop control of the body** – equipment should be chosen carefully to reflect the size of the outdoor area and the amount of storage space available. Practitioners need to choose equipment which offers children the chance to develop control of different parts of their bodies. This includes opportunities for them to: develop their arm strength through pulling, pushing and rolling such things as large balls or barrels; to balance; to gain spatial awareness and first hand experience of what it feels like to be up, under, over, inside or round; to develop skills in using specific equipment such as balls, bats, bean bags, hoops; and to learn to control wheeled vehicles such as bikes, scooters and push/pull-along carts and wagons. When choosing wheeled vehicles, it is advisable to select at least some which can be ridden by more than one child. This encourages collaborative and co-operative play and helps children develop skills of negotiation. Traffic signs can be bought or made by the children and obstacle courses, such as weaving between traffic cones, can be set up. Advice should always be taken from local health and safety advisers when considering installing climbing equipment
- **creative resources** – outdoors it is possible to engage with art on a large scale; painting on large sheets of paper with large brushes or rollers, making rubbings or prints, making collage pictures or patterns

with petals, leaves, twigs, small logs, stones, shells or conkers, chalking on the playground or blackboard attached to the wall, weaving long plastic or crepe paper strips through fencing. Similarly music can be louder and more collaborative; children can perform in a marching band using percussion instruments, explore a music sculpture such as a frame with various items including metal or wooden tubes, saucepan lids, old CDs attached for beating, dance to taped music perhaps wearing ankle and wrist bells and dressing up clothes, or learn new action songs and ring games. A wooden pallet can be covered and used to make a low stage so that children can perform for their friends

- **resources to encourage scientific and mathematical exploration** – robust magnifiers, binoculars, cameras to record seasonal changes, and gardening equipment are essential to enable children to explore the outdoor world. Clipboards with paper and pencils or crayons will encourage observational drawing. Concave and convex mirrors can be attached to walls, and items which reflect the light, such as prisms can be hung from trees. Resource collections are useful for exploring seasonal changes. A windy day box could include streamers, a wind-sock, flags, a kite, bubble mixture and blowers, windmills, wind chimes and relevant story books, whilst a rainy day box could include various types of fabric and plastic straws to make and test umbrellas, waterproof jackets and trousers, umbrellas, rain gauge to measure the rainfall plus relevant story books. Having boxes organised in advance enables practitioners to respond spontaneously and exploit current interests. No-one can plan that on Monday the force of the wind will be explored first-hand; the opportunity has to be grabbed when it arises. Children can only learn about the weather by experiencing it; they do not learn about snow by sticking cotton wool on paper! Other resource collections could include things for looking through, things which roll, things with wheels and things which bounce. Large bucket scales, robust tape measures or metre rulers can be provided to encourage measurement and comparisons

- **books** – to encourage children to refer to books as they engage in outdoor learning, practitioners should make available a small book box or trolley containing a variety of non-fiction and fiction books relevant to the outdoor environment. This could be permanently situated near the quiet area so that children know where to go when they want to discover more about a creature they have found or share a story with a friend

Storage is obviously a big consideration and many early years settings do not have adequate storage facilities to enable them to collect an inspiring range of resources. A large storage shed with shelving is essential. Lock-up garages are useful in areas where vandalism is a problem. Smaller equipment could be stored in containers and trolleys with wheels to facilitate tidying away. These containers and their sections should be clearly labelled so that children can see where things belong and are able to put back what they have used. During a session they should be positioned near to the appropriate part of the play area for example, the small physical equipment such as bats, balls and quoits should be sited near the ball play area. Those settings with small areas may only have one or two storage trolleys with trays; the contents of the trays could be changed on different days to offer a range of experience over time. Any resource box collections should have an easy to check inventory so that whoever uses them can check items back at the end of session and replace any missing items.

Practitioners supporting children's outdoor learning

All adults working with young children need to understand the importance of outdoor experience and be enthusiastic about getting involved with the children outside. Positive attitudes are essential. The outdoor area is not just a place to let off steam; it is a place where a whole curriculum can be offered. Adults provide powerful role models for young children. Both boys and girls need to see men and women engaging in the full range of outdoor experiences. It is important to challenge stereotypical views, therefore women need to be seen playing such things as football or chasing games, and men need to be seen engaged in such things as carefully handling and observing a small creature or taking part in preparing food for a picnic.

Planning for outdoor learning is essential. The importance of planning the environment and resources carefully to ensure that children can access a wide range of experiences has already been outlined.

When practitioners are planning what the children will be learning during a particular week or day, they need to make sure they have identified outdoor as well as indoor opportunities. The same learning objective needs to be offered in a range of different ways to support the variety of preferred learning styles within the group. Some children will access learning objectives more enthusiastically out of doors than they would if asked to work at an indoor table-top activity. It is often difficult, because of the unpredictability of the weather, to plan exactly when a particular learning experience is to be offered outside. However, if the outdoor opportunities are listed next to the relevant learning objectives, practitioners can decide on a day-to-day basis when to offer them. It may also be useful to have a sheet on which to record the spontaneous learning that takes place out of doors; so much happens outside which has not been specifically planned for. Practitioners who find they have been involved in a small group's learning could jot down briefly what they did and what learning this promoted. In this way learning which arises from children's spontaneous interests can be valued in the planning process.

In the same way as they do indoors, practitioners need to plan cross-curricular experiences outside. Making the provision suggested will offer children the chance to engage with all aspects of learning, but adults need to plan to get involved. This can either be through providing opportunities and resources, undertaking observations or in direct involvement in experiences with a specific focus to extend children's ideas and learning. Experiences which adults could plan to be involved with include:

- organising parachute games, group games such as 'What's the time Mr Wolf?' and ring games such as 'Here we go round the mulberry bush'
- modelling use of egg timers or other mechanical timers to enable children to time turns on favourite equipment
- setting up obstacle courses to promote a sense of achievement and develop physical skills
- taking the children on a focused walk in the local community to:
    - look at the natural world to promote a sense of awe and wonder and to model vocabulary of the outdoor world, including such things as names of creatures, mini-beasts and weather.

- encourage questioning and use of descriptive language and comparative language
- look for print, numbers, shapes, signs and symbols, or readers and writers in the environment
- find out about design features of buildings and other structures
- make comparisons between old and new buildings
- discuss types of buildings and who lives or works in them
- carry out vehicle surveys
- discover the uses of information and communication technology in the environment, such as which button to press when crossing the road, traffic lights, screens at railway or bus stations showing train or bus times
- gain first hand experience to support role-play; a visit to the fire station before setting up fire-fighter role-play

- putting up signs around the outdoor area such as directions to find the lost teddy
- playing in role-play areas modelling use of language associated with different roles and of relevant reading and writing materials
- encouraging children to make chalk roadways or maps on the ground
- modelling a range of physical skills such as running, hopping, skipping, jumping, climbing, balancing, throwing, catching, dancing to taped music
- encouraging children to refine skills by suggesting physical challenges such as aiming a bean bag at the letter snake or number line and offering challenges like 'Can you throw the beanbag onto the first letter of your name, or into a bucket?' 'Can you walk with the bean-bag on your head?' 'Can you kick or throw the ball to a named person in the circle?' 'Can you carry out a sequence of movements such as 3 jumps and 2 hops?'
- setting up and directing children round traffic systems to encourage more controlled use of wheeled vehicles
- encouraging children to be aware of physical changes in their bodies during exercise

- encouraging children to count things such as shoots in the garden, jumps across the grass or paving slabs, skittles knocked down, legs on mini-beasts
- helping children to carry out surveys such as birds using the bird table, children using a piece of equipment, or red cars going past
- focussing on language of position; high, low, up, down, under, over, through, when children are using climbing equipment
- setting up pulley systems
- exploring forces using wheeled toys, see-saws or rockers, and by testing cars on slopes with different surfaces or gradients
- drawing round and measuring length of shadows at different times of day
- using collections of natural materials such as leaves or shells for sorting, matching, ordering in different ways such as by length or weight, and counting
- suggesting construction challenges, for example, 'Can you build a bridge for the Three Billy Goats to cross?' or 'a roof that the wolf can't blow down?'

It should be clear by now that the role of the adult out of doors is the same as indoors. Practitioners need to have an overview of the whole environment, but also need to be able to work on focused experiences with small groups of children. Time for outdoor learning needs to be allocated to enable children to work on projects in depth. Ideally children should be offered the chance to move freely between the indoor and outdoor areas for a good part of the session. This enables them to plan and manage their own time and to integrate indoor and outdoor learning. Where children all have to go outside at the same time and only have a short period out of doors, their experience is largely one of letting off steam. This is because the area becomes too crowded, staff are reduced to supervising rather than getting involved and there is insufficient time for children to develop their ideas. In this situation practitioners need to plan times when a small group can go outside to work in more depth with an adult.

Practitioners also need to observe and assess children learning out of doors. Some children will show evidence of higher level ability outside than would be seen indoors. In order to gain a complete view of children's learning it is essential to note outdoor achievements and interests. Many practitioners use post-it notes to jot down interesting things children do or say. These are dated and, along with indoor jottings, stuck into the child's early learning profile under the relevant area of development, quickly building up a record of the child's progress to share with parents.

How can parents help?

Parents can offer many of the resources and opportunities suggested for practioners. They need to consider how much outdoor experience their child gets in a typical week, and liase with staff at the early years setting their child attends to ensure and insist that there is enough outdoor provision. Parents need to think about how they can offer even more. For example, if they tend to go everywhere by car, extra time could be allocated for walking to some nearby places. Time could be set aside each week to visit the nearest local park or recreation ground. Parents should encourage older and younger family members and friends to play together so that each group learns from the other.

Parents need to ensure that their children are suitably clothed for the important outdoor experiences they should be having at their early years setting. Warm outer clothing and sturdy footwear with non-slip soles are essential, and children should be unrestricted by clothing when climbing or riding wheeled toys; tracksuits are ideal. Children should also not have the pressure of worrying about getting messy. Years ago, before the widespread use of washing machines, washing had to be done by hand and yet parents then were much less worried about mess. Children who have been told not to get dirty will be inhibited and restricted in their outdoor learning. It is better to dress children in old clothes which can withstand a bit of mud or grass.

Additionally, parents can try to find time in busy schedules to take their children at weekends or for holidays to outdoor spaces that are not always accessible to practitioners. This often includes local recreation grounds and parks including country parks, woods or forests, nature reserves, the seaside, moors and mountains. They will observe their child's awe and wonderment when faced with vast stretches of open space. They will also see how much more readily children settle to their own projects in an open space, for example, the child on the edge of the sea filling his bucket and emptying the water onto the sand over and over again.

Parents, like practitioners, need to recognise that outdoor experience is absolutely essential for their child's healthy development and learning. Playing out of doors with their children lays the foundation for a healthy future and increases children's intellectual capacity. It can also bring back happy memories of parents their own childhood play.

Conclusion

The great outdoors has much to offer both adults and children. In recent years children's experience of being outside has been restricted and concern has been expressed about the effect of this on children's health and development. Parents and practitioners now need to work together to ensure that children are offered their full entitlement of stimulating and enjoyable outdoor experiences.

There is no doubt that healthy human development, including social, emotional, physical and intellectual aspects, depends on children getting outside experiences which can be solitary or with others.

Experiences offered to children are likely to differ from those adults remember from their own childhood, but with determination and commitment to developing children's learning through outdoor provision they will become close.

Useful contacts for advice and resources

Local authority health and safety adviser and/or adviser for development of grounds/play areas

Brian Clegg, *for wheeled toys, storage trolleys etc.*
Slackcote Mill, Slackcote Lane, Delph, Oldham, OL3 5TP Tel: 01457 875881
Community Playthings, *for hollow blocks, wooden climbing materials and robust wheeled toys etc.*
Robertsbridge, East Sussex TN32 5DR Tel: 0800 387457
Compton Buildings Ltd., *for lock up storage garages*
Station Works, Fenny Compton, Southam, Warwickshire CV47 2XB
Tel: 01295 770291 www.comptongarages.com
GLS Dudley, *for A-Frames, planks, climbing equipment, small equipment etc.*
1 Mollison Avenue, Enfield EN3 7XQ Tel: 0208 805 8333
Learning Through Landscapes, *a national charity which can advise on how to develop outdoor areas and possible funding sources*
Third Floor, Southside Offices, The Law Courts, Winchester SO23 9DL
Tel: 01962 846258 www.ltl.org.uk
NES/Arnold, *for climbing and balancing equipment, small apparatus, gardening equipment, wheeled toys, etc.*
Ludlow Hill Road, West Bridgford, Nottingham NG2 6H9 Tel: 0115 9717700
www.nesarnold.co.uk
Timberline Ltd., *for playground equipment*
Highlands Place Foxwood Industrial Park, Foxwood Road, Sheepbridge, Chesterfield S41 9RN www.timberline.co.uk

Further reading and resource books

Bayley, R. & Broadbent, L. (2001) *50 Exciting Things To Do Outside* West Midlands: Lawrence Educational Publications
Bilton, H. (1998) *Outdoor Play in the Early Years* London: David Fulton
Bradford Education (1995) *Can I Play Out?* Bradford Education Authority
Featherstone, S. (2001) *The Little Book of Outdoor Play* Leicestershire: Featherstone Education Ltd.
Goldschmied, E. & Jackson, S. (1994) *People Under Three* London: Routledge
Early Education (1998) *Learning for Life* London: Early Education & Boots Company
Early Education (2000) *Living, Loving & Learning* London: Early Education & Boots Company
Lindon, J. (1999) *Too Safe for Their Own Good* London: National Early Years Network
Ouvry, M. (2000) *Exercising Muscles and Minds* London: National Early Years Network

Storybooks for children

There are lots of books which give children images of outdoors. These include books with images of people who work outside, who play sport outside and images of geographical outdoor features as well as different countries. There are also many stories which have outdoor settings. Bookshops and libraries will give advice. Here are just a few suggestions.

Bears in the Night by Stan and Jan Berenstain, Collins ISBN 0-0017-1271-3

Charlie's House by Reviva Schermbruker & Niki Daly, Walker Books ISBN 0-7445-2394-X

Cowboy Baby by Sue Heap, Walker Books ISBN 0-7445-6330-5

It's the Bear by Jez Alborough, Walker Books ISBN 0-7445-4385-1

Little Beaver and The Echo by Amy MacDonald and Sarah Fox-Davies, Walker Books ISBN 0-7445-231-X

Our Puppy's Holiday by Ruth Brown, Anderson Press ISBN 0-86264-145-4

Percy The Park Keeper series by Nick Butterworth, Picture Lions

Rosie's Walk by Pat Hutchins, Bodley Head Children's Books ISBN 0-370-32446-3

Roxaboxen by Alice McLeran and Barbara Cooney, Lothrop, Leeds & Shepard Books ISBN 0-6880-7592-4

The Last Cowboys (and others in the series) by Harry Horse, Puffin Books ISBN 0-14-130028-0

The Obvious Elephant by Bruce Robinson & Sophie Windham, Bloomsbury Paperbacks ISBN 0747550786

Three Billy Goats Gruff Traditional, First Favourite Tales, Ladybird Books ISBN 0-72149-736-5

We're Going on a Bear Hunt by Michael Rosen and Helen Oxenbury, Walker Books ISBN 0-7445-5572-8

Where the Wild Things Are by Maurice Sendak, Picture Lions ISBN 0-00-664086-9

Wombat Goes Walkabout by Michael Morpurgo and Christian Birmingham, Picture Lions ISBN 0-0064-627-1

Books with stimulating outdoor images

Goldsworthy, A. (1989) *Wall* London: Thames and Hudson Ltd.
Goldsworthy, A. (1990) *Parklands* Middlesex: Viking
Goldsworthy, A. (1994) *Stone* Middlesex: Viking
Goldsworthy, A. (1996) *Wood* Middlesex: Viking
Goldsworthy, A. (2000) *Time* London: Viking
Smit, T. (2001) *Eden* London: Transworld Publishers